MY PURPOSE - SERIES

I0540536

What kind of

leader am I?

Assisting leaders in rediscovering
how leadership is meant to be

EUNICE ANITA

The Netherlands

What kind of leader am I?

MY PURPOSE-SERIES
Copyright © 2019 Eunice Anita
Published by Highly Favored Publishing
www.highlyfavored.nl

Editing by Duvilène Pieter
Cover illustration © 2019 Highly Favored Publishing
Book Layout © 2019 Highly Favored Publishing

Motivational
Paperback ISBN 978-94-92266-18-7
E-Book Epub ISBN 978-94-92266-19-4
NUR 707, 740, 808
BASIC BUS071000, REL108030

Contents

Introduction

There is a famous saying stating that there can be only one captain to a ship. So, here on earth, a company has one Chief Executive Officer (CEO), a school has one principal, and a church has one head pastor. Often times, some people called and chosen as leaders, in business as well as in congregational context, have a tendency of operating from a controlling and almost manipulative stance. This often has nothing to do with the way they want to work but with fear of failing as a leader, and because of the tricks and scams of the religious spirit who is trying to destroy the leaders and their divine mandate.

The leader who functions and operates from the knowledge of who he/she is in Christ, has nothing to be afraid of. Many know this, but the way of providing guidance and the way they put leadership into practice, does not reflect the aforementioned.

This booklet is meant as a helping hand for you, leader, for those moments in which you need to refocus on your call as a leader.

The Bible teaches us that many are called, but few are chosen. Dear leader, for you to function and operate as the leader that God has called and chosen you to be, you must remind yourself continuously of who you are in Christ.

Affirming statements

God gave me a portion of faith, and my priority is to use it so it can multiply. With this in mind, I declare that,

\# I am created in the image and likeness of God.

\# I am a human being with a divine purpose in business, ministry, or both.

\# I have accepted my calling as a leader, and I understand that God is putting or will put me through a process to let the diamond which He has placed in me shine bright.

\# I make use of the authority given to me, but I do not think of myself more highly than others.

\# I am not searching for power, but instead, I want to serve in the areas entrusted to me.

\# I understand that being a leader does not mean being manipulative and control freak.

\# I lead by example, also in terms of apologizing when applicable.

I consist of a body, soul, and spirit, and it is essential to nourish them all.

Although I am rational in the natural, I walk in faith, knowing that the Lord is by my side.

I put the full armor of God on daily.

Leadership is rooted in God

Leadership, like everything else, was designed by the Lord God, Creator of all. God put Adam in charge as the leader in the garden of Eden. Could it be that because of bad management the snake got hold of Eve and his evil plan had a chance to be executed?

In the story of Moses and Jethro, we can read about another model of leadership, which was approved by the Lord. Jethro gave advice to Moses, but at all times he emphasized for Moses to consult with the Lord.

Especially in the books of 1 Kings, 2 Kings, 1 Chronicles, and 2 Chronicles, we can identify the spiritual and natural leadership as instituted by the Lord. The kings were the natural leaders of a nation while the prophets were the spiritual leaders, they were the voice of the Lord here on earth. These two types of leadership still exist today. The natural leader is not only at the level of nations but exists also at the level of businesses and families.

The spiritual leader is still as vital as it was in the time of the Bible for, we need to hear the Word and the Voice of the Lord.

Prayer

Lord God, thank you for providing us with a structure of leadership based on which we can construct and build businesses, communities, and families that honor You. Jesus, we invite You to come and guide each and every person that You have called as a leader or as part of Your five-fold leadership team in Your Body, and/or as a leader in either their house, their business or in their community.

Father help us to be open for the bits of advice of the people You send on our way to help us. For this, we need the discernment that only You can provide to us because the enemy may also send wrong advice and hope on our path.

Holy Spirit, I invite you to be at my side day and night and reveal to me the ways of the Father, in Jesus' Name, Amen.

Scripture

Genesis 1:26; Exodus 18:14, 17-24; Ephesians 4:11-13; 2 Timothy 2:15

Called as a leader

Being a leader means carrying a burden that does not go away or vanish overnight. Jesus had a responsibility that only He could bear. He alone was anointed for that. Can you imagine what would have happened if a man purely of flesh and blood had to go through all the trials and tribulations which Jesus went thru? So, it is also in the case of leadership. Being seen in the eyes of man as a leader might seem and feel as important, but the main question is, can I carry the burden that the position brings with it?

If you are called and anointed by God as a leader, all the burden that the position brings with it, will feel as light as a feather, for Jesus will be the one carrying the weight for you. Jesus said: *"…Take my yoke…for my yoke is easy"*. (Matthew 11:29-30, CJB) The main point is to let the Lord lead you and show you in which area you are called to lead. It might be in business, ministry, family, politics, you name it. Be the leader God called you to be.

Lord, You Who have called me as a leader, I invite You to be in control of my process. I admit that I cannot do this on my own. Some processes and situations seem strange, and at times, I doubt it has to do with You. At times I think that it is not You, but I must admit, once again, that Your ways are not my ways.

Jesus, help me in the process of understanding that I must be molded for the level(s) of authority that the Father wants to entrust me with. Lord, as Your Word teaches me that there is a time for everything, I know that there is a time of being molded and formed into the vessel You want for me to be. So, I know also that there is a time when the vessel shall be ready and will be put in use for Your glory and honor. Lord, guide me through the processes of being and staying the vessel You formed.

I thank You, Father, that You take away all fear of failure as a leader from me and that You are guiding me on every step of this road. Holy Spirit I invite You to stay at my side every day in the Name of Jesus, Amen.

Scriptures

Ecclesiastes 3:1; 2 Timothy 4:7-8; 1 Peter 5: 1-5

Influence not power

When looking at the formal definition of influence and power, it can be noticed that (in theory), there is a fragile line between the two. Influence is described in an online dictionary of the Oxford University Press as *"The capacity to have an effect on the character, development, or behaviour of someone or something, or the effect itself."*[1] The word power is described as *"The capacity or ability to direct or influence the behaviour of others or the course of events."*[2]

Shortly said, both mean having an effect on the behavior of others. The question would then be, what kind of leader do I want to be? One that acts from the stance of influence or one that leads from the attitude of power?

In contrary to the minor difference in the formal definition, is there a considerable difference between the words influence and power when looking at them form an emotional and social perspective.

---

[1] https://www.lexico.com/en/definition/influence
[2] https://www.lexico.com/en/definition/power

Influence is often associated with a gentler and little to no-pressure way of motivating someone to do something. Power, on the other hand, is emotionally and socially, associated with intimidation.

Would God want leaders to guide and lead from a position of intimidation? Or would He be glad about a leader that is empathetic yet knows to use his/her authority when a situation requires this?

From the viewpoint of an employee, team member or church member, which leadership style would work as inspiring, motivating, and not frightening? Which leadership style would intimidate others? Which leadership style would not make them feel as if they are slaves?

God could have used His power when sin was committed in the garden of Eden, but He chose to handle with mercy and grace. Be a leader that balances authority with kindness and sympathy.

Prayer

Heavenly Father, thank you for setting an example as a leader. Jesus Christ, thank you for showing us how a leader here on earth can work together with his/her team. Holy Spirit, I invite you to come and guide me on my journey of becoming a better leader. I want to resemble You, the Divine Trinity, in my leadership style. Help me to respect others the way I want them to respect me and help me to guide, inspire, and lead others in a righteous way so we all can experience Your blessings. I thank You in Jesus' Name, Amen.

Scriptures

Matthew 7:12; John 3:30; Galatians 6:9; Philippians 2:3

Being a servant

It was usual to have a servant in the Biblical time. The one having a servant was called a master though the relationship between the two could be categorized more like a slave and master one.[3] So, one could say having no servant(s), meant not being a master. If we translate this to the terms of leader and team, it would mean having no team is equal to not being a leader. In modern society, we have been taught, almost to the point of being indoctrinated, that one should aim to become the leader and make sure not to be a servant. Can there be a leader without a servant?

There is a difference in being a servant and being treated to the bone as a servant. Sadly enough, the latter happens today to the extent of making people slaves again. People are not locked up by physical chains or in small cabins anymore, but they experience or feel mental or spiritual handcuffs or chains on their feet. This situation

---

[3] SLAVES AND SERVANTS IN THE TIME OF JESUS - HISTORY AND CULTURE, American Bible Society, http://bibleresources. americanbible.org/resource/slaves-and-servants-in-the-time-of-jesus-history-and-culture, accessed July 2019

may easily lead to burnouts. The leader is often, not always, the one responsible for the pressure the person is feeling.

Let us take a look at the concept of being a leader and at the same time, a servant. Looking at things and experiencing them from both sides, makes it easier for a leader in bringing balance. The most excellent example of what being a leader means was spoken about by and shown by Jesus Christ Himself. He told his disciples: "...*On the contrary, whoever among you wants to be a leader must become your servant, and whoever wants to be first must be your slave! For the Son of Man did not come to be served, but to serve - and to give his life as a ransom for many.*" (Matthew 20:26-28, CJB)

Jesus washed the feet of His disciples while they were the ones following Him and serving Him. Can you, as a modern-day leader put this example into practice? You don't have to wash the feet of your family, employee, or congregants, but when the pressure is high, they would surely appreciate a helping hand. Be (at times) creative in the ways to show your fellows that you do care about them and that you value them as much as they value you. Show them that you are a servant too.

Prayer

Jesus Christ, thank you for setting an excellent example for me to follow. I am committed to setting forth a good example in all areas of my life, and I invite You, Holy Spirit, to come and help me with this matter. I do not consider it to be a loss to be equal to my fellows for even You, Jesus Christ, Who had all the right to think so, had not thought and acted that way. Father, I am your humble servant in the areas that you have entrusted me with. I pray in Jesus' Name, Amen.

Scriptures

Matthew 20:26-28;   Mark 10:42-45; Philippians 2:5-9

Failing as part of the process

The fact that at times you do or get things wrong does not make you a failure. It is merely a sign that you are human. The moment that someone cannot admit that he or she has failed, it all becomes a problem. And, when that person has a leadership position, it becomes a bigger problem.

It is crucial for a leader to lead by example. If a leader's attention is drawn by another person to indicate that the leader had done something wrong, the leader should not let pride take control of him/her and disregard the remark as a sign of disrespect. On the other hand, the person indicating the situation should do so with due respect, but not with fear.

As a leader, one should not be afraid of making mistakes. The Scriptures teach us that a righteous falls seven times and rises up again. When he/she rises, it will be with more knowledge and wisdom. The Lord teaches and strengthens His children thru life situations, so do not think that when things get tricky that the Lord is not involved. At times He might not be involved, but there will be moments in which He is. That will be not to forsake you when you fail, but rather to mold you so you may become the ideal pot of clay in His hands.

Prayer

Father, I admit that I am not perfect. I acknowledge that I may fail as a leader and as a person. But above all, I know that with You living in me all will be well. You have forgiven me my transgressions and are molding me into a leader to impact the world for the better.

Holy Spirit, I invite you to be at my side and help me withstand the spirit of pride and control that can impede me to identify and admit my faults. Jesus Christ, You who have overcome all of the evil on the earth, I come to You knowing that You want to abide in me and help me in every step of growing and becoming the leader the Father has called me to be. Thank you for Your mercy Father in Jesus' Name I pray, Amen.

Scriptures

Proverbs 24:16; 1 John 4:18

Saying I am sorry

It is remarkable that when we are in the role of citizen, man or woman, parents, neighbors, relatives or friends, we have no problem to say I am sorry when we have done something wrong, missed something or just failed in whatever sense of the word. Why is it than that when a man or a woman is in the role of leader, he/she has an issue with saying I am sorry when it is appropriate to say so. Why? I am not talking about hypothetical cases but situations that I have experienced and heard too much about.

Some would look for the answer in the psychological atmosphere and others in the personality type. I want to challenge you to combine those point of views with the emotional and spiritual one.

The society, locally and internationally, has grown to model a leader as the one person that is always right, the one that never fails. The reality is that only Jesus Christ was impeccable. All of us have one or more flaws, and there is no shame in admitting this.

Some have been wrongly convinced that admitting flaws would mean losing respect from others. This is one of the wrong thinking patterns, which I believe is rooted in the evil works of the enemy who wants to destroy the work of the Lord.

When the Lord called you as a leader, He knew that you will fail and/or make mistakes. That was no reason for Him to disqualify you as a leader. Why do you think than that admitting that you are human, and humans do make mistakes, would disqualify you as a leader?

Dare to admit when you are or were wrong and see how the Lord Himself will make the relationship and the mutual respect between you, as a leader, and the brethren much stronger. Be and act like a matured leader. A leader who knows his/her divine purpose.

Prayer

Lord, I admit that I am a sinner and that you washed and purified me with the blood of Jesus Christ. I acknowledge that my flesh is sinful and that I need your help in the continuous fight of overcoming the flesh.

Thank you, Lord, that in my mistakes you correct me and that I can always admit that I am not perfect, but He that lives in me is.

Holy Spirit, I invite you to be at my side and to guide me in all that I do. When I exclude You from my decisions and act on myself, and make mistakes, help me to identify and admit my faults and not to look for excuses.

I know that You are the Lord of grace and forgiveness. I will not seek to commit errors, but when they happen, I will repent and ask You for forgiveness. I can rest assured that You will forgive me my faults, and so should I forgive myself, and all who were involved should and will do so because of the love of Jesus. In Jesus' Name, I pray, Amen.

Scriptures

Proverbs 14:9; 1 Corinthians 13:11; Ephesians 4:32; James 5:16

A great team

Leadership is defined in an online dictionary as *the activity of leading an organization or a group of people or the ability to do so.*[4] Another helpful definition we found for leadership states that *it is the art of achieving a goal by motivating a group of people to act towards completion of the common goal.*[5] The point is that for there to be leadership, there must be a group consisting of at least two persons. When one is alone, there is no need for leadership.

For the leader and the leadership skills in you to be developed, there must be a group for you to guide. There are numerous examples in sports and business were the leader was the binding factor leading the team to victory. Individually, the team members might not be the most capable, brightest or strongest, but if the Lord has entrusted you with a team, know that He has given you Jesus Christ as the cornerstone of your

---

[4] http://www.businessdictionary.com/definition/leadership.html

[5] Susan Ward, March 2019, https://www.thebalancesmb.com/leadership-definition-2948275

team. Trust in the Lord, and He will make your team a great team, a winning team.

Prayer

Heavenly Father, thank you for helping me understand and accept that you created us, humans, with different sets of physical and mental capabilities. Not for us to look down on each other but for us to complement each other so together, we can be a great team. Father, just as you team up with Jesus Christ, the Holy Spirit and Your host of angels, help us, the leaders, to follow our example and be a team together with those you entrusted to us for us to lead.

Holy Spirit, I invite you to come and help me to be the leader that the Father has called me to be. Help me to be like the head of a human body which thinks and gives directions to all parts of the body. Jesus Christ, abide in me and create in me a heart that is tender and loving, yet strict and with authority when required, towards my team(s). I pray in Jesus' Name. Amen.

Scriptures

Proverbs 11:14; 1 Corinthians 12: 20-25; 1 Peter 4:10

Delegate and trust

At times, being the one in charge of a business, a department, a section or team, the idea might come up that it is better for yourself to do some tasks because you don't have time to guide or teach others how to execute those tasks. When there is time to guide and teach others, you do so. You could also choose to keep all the knowledge for yourself and all the consequences thereof.

Another scenario would be that at times, you nicely delegate tasks to others, and then the circus starts. You start harassing the people to whom you entrusted the tasks because they are not doing it the way you want it or the moment you want it done. The minimum change compared to when you used to do the task, you disapprove without taking some time to evaluate the modifications to see if they are for the better. Shortly said, you become totally upset and negative. Why?

Could it be that the feeling of losing control is coming up, and you don't know how to deal with it? Could it be that the enemy is telling you that others can do the job better than you and you think: *impossible, no one is better than me!*

Take a close look at your body. Though the head is the one that comes up with ideas, it must delegate the execution of the plans to primarily the feet, to take the body to the place of action, and secondly the hands to perform the work. Organizations function the same way.

The growth of an organization, being business or ministry, is mainly dependent on delegating tasks, including the related authority, effectively.

Delegating does not mean losing oversight. It means trusting the Lord before, during, and after delegating the tasks. It means trusting that He is the One guiding you and the person to whom you are transferring authority.

Be the leader that foster growth of the team members, the entity in general, and himself by delegating tasks effectively. Monitoring progress and providing feedback in a constructive way, are part of an effective and efficient delegation process. Monitoring at no time or moment means harassing. Plan and monitor effectively and always be realistic in your expectations.

Prayer

Heavenly Father, I give You thanks for all that You have done and will continue to do for me. Father, being and acting as a leader means bearing responsibilities which at times can be overwhelming, especially when not feeling comfortable with delegating authority to others. Jesus Christ, I ask You to help me in the process of finding the right balance in delegating tasks to others and executing them on my own.

Holy Spirit, I invite You to come and assist me with monitoring and providing constructive feedback to others by speaking the truth in love. I recognize that people are different in character and so also in the way that they feel comfortable with when being approached. Help me to not overwhelm people with critics yet, on the other hand, not to be too softy, causing loss of respect as a leader. Holy Spirit, help me to be the leader the Father called me to be. I want to love, motivate, speak, and when necessary, give a reprimand under Your guidance. Assist me so I can be a leader that honors the Father and those the Father entrusted him with. My trust is in the Father, the Son, and the Holy Spirit, Amen.

Scriptures

Proverbs 15:13; Proverbs 19:20; Ephesians 4:12,15; 2 Timothy 2:2

Weighing the load

Being a leader means, besides all the aspects of the responsibility of ensuring and making things are done, that you take care of and protect your team members. Sometimes you must protect the team members from themselves, or better said, from their ambition of growing fast and being seen by others. At other times you must protect them from yourself because you are the leader who needs and wants the work completed as soon as possible.

How can you protect your team members from yourself? That is by weighing the load.

Although leaders (might) show empathy, often times some seem to forget or do disregard the reality in which a team member or some team members are operating. This might be in the sense of the spread of the workload among the team members, insufficient capacity in man-hours and/or expectations which were set to high. Striving at times is no problem. It becomes a problem when it heads on the road of getting structural and leading to extreme disturbance in the balance between work (or responsibility in congregation) and private life. Directing and/or redirecting some specific tasks to a small or select group of team members, just because you think that they can do it better, might lead over time to an unequal or even false yoke on the shoulder of these team members. This also limits the growth opportunity for the other team members.

As a leader, one should make sure that the team members can function well. In order to do so, the team members must be able to rest well, take enough pauses, and be happy. By being alert on and taking actions with regards to the heaviness of the load resting on your team, you are already helping them. Actually, you are helping yourself, because the burden on them is also on you and in its fullness.

A leader who has happy and motivated team members does achieve more than a leader with a team of exhausted people. The latter group is less efficient and effective in their performance.

Take care of your team! Take care of yourself! It is better to plan and later adjust the planning or the expectations than to have disappointing results and loose team members along the way for the wrong reasons. After all, we make plans, but the purposes as defined by The Lord will prevail.

Prayer

Heavenly Father, I come before You, humble and as I am, to recognize that I need You in my life. Father, I want to be the leader You called me to be, and for this, I need Your help. Jesus Christ, help me to be a leader that stays alert on the weight of labor that is sent down thru me towards my team members. Help me to take care of them and of myself by addressing the factors that influence the workload negatively; if applicable, also with those higher up in the organization. Let my light rise in the darkness.

Holy Spirit, I invite You to come and help me withstand the enemy and his tactics of putting a yoke of oppression on and talking bad with team members. Help me to create an atmosphere in which my team members can function well and be able to grow and bloom. I pray in Jesus Mighty Name, Amen.

Scriptures

1 Kings 12:4; Proverbs 19:21; Isaiah 58: 9-12; Matthew 11:29-30; 1 Corinthians 3:5-7

Pulling down the spirit of control

A hypernym that can be used for *being a leader* is being responsible. Responsibility and authority are interdependent. The more responsibility, the more authority.

The enemy of our soul, who comes as a lion to seek who he can devour, has been using tactics and tricks to limit leaders and the organizations that they are leading. How? By releasing anxiety, doubt, and fear.

One person cannot do all the tasks and bear all the responsibilities in an organization. That is why there are levels of leadership with the corresponding level of teams. Responsibility and authority are delegated downwards, and accountability flows up. When delegating authority, there must be a level of acceptance that the person to whom it is transferred is matured and able to act with a sound mind.

What does the enemy do? He plants weeds of anxiety and doubt, which makes the leader nervous and thinking that the persons to whom responsibility and authority were delegated cannot do the job right. He plants weeds of fear which makes leaders at the lower and mid-level, and even those at the top, to think that agreements made (within the organization and with externals), cannot be honored because of the poor performance of those below him/her in the organization.

Shortly said, the leader will start to think that he/she will fail on all levels and in all areas. If and when the leader allows those dark thoughts to grow, an entry-point for the spirit of manipulation & control is created. Manipulation and control are two ways thru which the spirit of religion does manifest himself. Rick Joyner describes in his book *Overcoming the Religious Spirit*[6] some signs that indicate that a religious spirit is interfering in someone's behavior. One of the signs he mentions is: *the person will have a leadership style, which is bossy, overbearing and intolerant of the weakness or failure of others.*

Take some time and reflect on these words. Take some time and evaluate your behavior as a leader. Please, do not condemn yourself but use it as a learning point and identification of the

---

[6] Overcoming the Religious Spirit (1996), page 47, Rick Joyner, Morningstar Publishing

way the enemy has been using to limit you. Mind you, this is the same spirit that tried to murder Martin Luther, the man who God used to bring a revolution in his lifetime.[7] Martin had to overcome this spirit before he could become the reformer we all know today.

Being influenced by the spirit of religion has its consequences. One consequence is a leader who will start to act, guide, and lead others from a stance of *extreme* micromanaging. You get a leader who will expect respect and obedience but who never listen to others or accepts the ideas or opinion of others. Everything must be done in his/her way; otherwise, it is not good. A remark or a why-question will be seen or taken as an act of disobedience. The leader will not admit being wrong or having failed, not even on the smallest things. The team members might feel as if they are 'modern' slaves.

Some of the consequences of this situation will be a loss of confidence, doubts, and no more sense of responsibility among the team members. On the long run, this will lead to people moving elsewhere because they feel working with the leader is a lost cause.

---

[7] Gods generals The Roaring Reformers (2003), page 129, Robert Liardon, Whitaker House

The enemy refrains organizations from growing by attacking the leaders. Whether it be a business, social organization, or a congregation. It is a subtle attack that slowly slips in but can cause greater damages than the apparent attacks like continuous demon manifestations through others.

The way BWicker described the tactic of the religious spirit in his blog is very straight forward because it is as it. He stated: *When a religious spirit is influencing us, we replace the power of the Holy Spirit in our lives with religious activity. In fact, the religious spirit is Satan's answer for the Holy Spirit. The religious spirit so closely mimics the Holy Spirit that many sincere believers think the Holy Spirit is leading them when, in fact, it is really a religious spirit.*[8]

Leader, you are human, and you make mistakes. That is the reality. A bigger truth is that the Lord has forgiven you your trespasses. To protect you from the errors described in this chapter, you need a counseling body who can speak to you openly and honestly, and to whom you do listen.

---

[8] Overcoming Religious Spirits (2009), BWicker
https://www.riverlifefellowship.com/overcoming-religious-spirits/

Your main counseling body is the Holy Spirit. But, at times, you will need a man of flesh and blood to confront you, in love, with the reality, because the spirit of religion interferes in your communication with the Holy Spirit.

Pull down the spirit of control. Pull down the spirit of manipulation. Pull down the spirit of religion and let the resurrected Jesus, The Messiah, rise up in you. You are called for greater things.

Prayer

Heavenly Father, I thank You for Your mercy and Your grace. You know how foolish I have been, yet You do not condemn me. Instead, You keep on loving me. Father, I confess my faults, mistakes, and sins in the area of leadership, and I know that You have forgiven me and have purified me from all wrongdoings. Thank you for making me stand firm in Jesus Christ.

Jesus Christ, I invite You to come and let Your righteousness shine like a sun in my heart, mind, and spirit. I long to be a caretaker of Your people, a caretaker who can plant seeds through business, ministry, and the community in general. I leave the responsibility and authority of giving water to the seeds to those called by You to do so. That way, we can work together in harmony and see how You provide growth.

Holy Spirit, I invite You to come and help me guard my heart and my mind from the attacks of the enemy. Be on me and in Me, and anoint me for the work in the area of leadership, in Jesus' Name. Amen.

Scriptures

Psalms 69:5; Proverbs 4:23; Proverbs 16:12; Hosea 10:12; Matthew 13:43; John 3:30; Hebrews 13:17; 1 Corinthians 3: 6-9

Wealth is more than money

When we hear the word wealth, we think instantly of money. Wealth is described in a dictionary as *the state of having much money or property*, or *as a large amount of something, i.e. ideas*.[9] It is also described as *having an abundant supply of possessions of value*[10] and *as tangible or intangible things that makes a person, family, or group better off*.[11]

What are your possessions? Which has (more) value for you, the tangible or the intangible ones?

What could be or is the wealth of a leader? Is it the number of people that follow him/her? Or, the impact that he/she is creating or making in the lives of those that listen and look up to him/her?

Whatever item, idea, feeling or thought that is or might be the most valuable to you, just make sure

---

[9] https://dictionary.cambridge.org/dictionary/english/wealth

[10] https://www.vocabulary.com/dictionary/ wealthy

[11] *Online Business Dictionary 2019.*
http://www.businessdictionary.com/definition/wealth.html

to make Jesus Christ the one above and at the center of your list of valuable things.

As a leader, make sure that your crown in heaven is being filled rather than focusing on accumulating wealth here on earth. The Lord is the One who provides earthly wealth for His children for He is the owner of silver and gold. Therefore, there is nothing wrong with having enough, financially speaking. The point is not to get attached to money or earthly wealth, which leads to neglecting the Source of everything or the instructions He is giving or will give in due time.

The enemy loves to use the trick of letting leaders focus on one wealth, being the number of followers they have. The spirit of pride is a liar and will always be. Greediness likes to accompany him, so they are on the same side.

The One everyone should follow, is Jesus Christ. If and when He is central in the minds and actions of men, including the leaders, there is no room for the enemy to make moves and destroy the purity of the blessings the Lord gives to His people. Value your blessings and your wealth, but above all, value Jesus Christ who died for you and has resurrected from the dead.

Prayer

Lord God, I thank you for the grace and mercy shown to me, my family, the business and/or congregation You entrusted me with. I admit that at times, I have thought of operating from the standpoint of what my eyes are seeing, and my ears have heard. Jesus Christ, I invite you to come and take hold of my mind, so the enemy can be kept out and not be able to influence my thinking when it comes to earthly wealth.

Heavenly Father, I know that You have promised that You will bless me and provide for me through the riches of glory in Jesus Christ. That is why I can declare that all my needs are supplied for, the tangible and the intangible ones.

Holy Spirit, I invite you to come and remind me every day that I am a child of the Heavenly King and that I have wealth here on earth as in heaven. Help me to (re)gain and possess the riches that the Father has assigned to me. Remind me, as often as necessary, that as a leader, called and chosen by the Most High, I can help others rearrange their priorities in terms of wealth accumulation. I pray in Jesus Mighty Name. Amen.

Scriptures

Jeremiah 29:11; John 14:16,17; 16:7,8

Notes

I want to encourage you to write down ideas, prayers, thoughts, plans, that which comes up in your mind when going through this booklet. Use it to encourage yourself as you walk in God's will through all phases of life.

About the author

Eunice is a professional with a master's degree in Accounting and Post-Master education in Auditing. After almost one and a half decade of working in the auditing and business sector, and having gained leadership experience in the corporate world, she took a leap of faith and started walking on two new roads, the road of entrepreneurship and spiritual growth. The latter required of her taking several steps of faith leading to a balanced and matured perspective on life, application of Biblical principles, the rationality of science and the combination of all together. As part of this process, she stepped into a leadership role in a congregational context. She is a professional that believes in the value of knowledge and skills as well as the importance of integrity, morality, sincerity, and unity. Knowledge sharing and helping others grow in their divine given purpose are also important to her. Therefore she dedicates time to coaching and teaching on leadership, financial management, and organizational management blended with relevant principles as described in the Bible.

She is the author of the book *Stories to tell to show His Greatness*, with the subtitle *God working thru the highly educated*. Furthermore, she served as editor of several manuscripts, including academic articles and thesis.

Other publications

Other booklets in the MY PURPOSE - Series

Can I achieve more in life?
Assisting man and woman rediscover their purpose in life
By Duvilène Pieter with Eunice Anita
Paperback ISBN 978-94-92266-16-3
E-Book Epub ISBN 978-94-92266-17-0

Who am I?
Assisting professionals regaining inner joy and peace
By Eunice Anita
Paperback ISBN 978-94-92266-14-6
E-Book Epub ISBN 978-94-92266-15-9

Other publications of the author

Stories to tell to show His Greatness
God working thru the highly educated
Paperback ISBN 978-15-04937-17-7
E-Book Epub ISBN 978-15-04937-18-4